Simple Money Making Ideas - Complete Business Ideas for Todays Entrepreneur

By

L J Samuels

Simple Money Making Methods that Pay You Over and Over Again

Contents

Introduction

Section 1

      5 Simple Money Making Machines

Section 2

      5 MORE Simple Money Making Machines

Section 3

      5 OFFLINE Money Making Machines

Introduction

This book is a compilation of three books I have written and published as Kindle books showing simple ways to make money from home.

Some are 'online' methods and some are 'offline' methods but all will make money.

A lot of my readers asked that I publish them as physical books for easier reference. So I decided to combine the three books into one – this one...

There is a reason for me not including a detailed 'contents' page. I would rather you read through the whole book rather than just 'cherry pick' from a 'contents' list. That way you have a better chance of seeing the potential of each method in order to choose the best ones for you.

You may be surprised at the simplicity of some of the methods that you had previously discounted thinking they are beyond your capabilities.

Every method in this book is tried and tested – most of them by me.

But every one of them is a *proven* method that will make you money if you take the time to implement them properly.

The number one reason people fail to make a living from home is lack of persistence.

They give up too soon.

"The difference between Success and Failure is not giving up." ~ Steven Redhead

In order to give yourself the best chance of making money with your chosen method, choose one or more that you think you will enjoy doing.

Choose one that you think will bring you some cash quickly; you will be surprised at how enthusiastic you are once you see that you can actually make some money.

My advice to you is to read through the book making notes of the methods that appeal to you.

Go back and read those methods again then choose the one that looks like one *you* can use to make you some extra cash,

Every person is different, so what looks easy to one person may be too difficult for others.

But, in this book, there will definitely be at least two or three methods that will suit YOU and make that extra cash you are aiming for.

From students to seniors, there will be at least a couple of methods that will make you money.

Please don't read this book then put it on the shelf and forget about it - **TAKE ACTION NOW!**

"Never Mistake Activity for Accomplishment"

~ L J Samuels

Section ONE

5 Simple Money Machines that Pay You Over and Over – After Doing the Work JUST ONE TIME

There are many ways to earn money online that only need a small financial investment to get started and even some that need NO INVESTMENT except your time and effort.

The ones that I am about to share with you should only require you to do the work ONE TIME, and could continue to send you **money month after month – for a long time**.

A lot of people overlook these simple money machines because they **don't** bring vast amounts of money right off the bat but **do** take time to set up, implement and promote before the money starts to come in – meaning **You Have to Do Some WORK to Get Started!**

"OMG, shock, horror – more work", I hear you say.

But think about it as speculating to accumulate; a few days work to get a few months (or more…) cash...

Some prefer to go with systems that require them to work every day so they can continue to produce an income. These people are exchanging work for cash –

6

they have to keep doing whatever it is that is producing their income or the money will STOP.

That's a fine thing to do – if you want a JOB.

But my vision of freedom is doing the work ONE TIME; then simply banking the cheques each month.

You see, I am basically a lazy person and have found it reasonably easy to make a living online by working hard for a while then kicking back and watching the money come in.

In fact I still get a monthly cheque for some things that I set up in 2009 and have not touched since.

How does that sound to you?

You can set up as many of these simple money machines as you like and still have the time to work any other money making methods you may want to be involved in.

None of the methods I am about to discuss are 'push button' methods – you will have to do the initial work and you may have to invest a small amount of money.

But you will only have to do it one time after which, if you have done it properly, you could be receiving cheques month after month after month etc…

These methods are scalable, which means that you can add to them and promote them allowing you to increase the amount of easy money you receive each month.

I urge you to remember that you will only get out what you put in.

What I mean by that is, if you read this and think; "that's great, I can do that", then you do absolutely nothing; that is exactly what you will get back – **a big, fat NOTHING!**

You have to take the time to set up your simple money machines correctly in order to receive money each month by doing the absolute minimum of work.

You also have to make sure that each method that you tackle is your **very best work**. Throwing together an incomplete, untested or badly written product will not produce the results that you want – so make it the very best that you possibly can!

Right, let's make a start…

Note: Read to the end of this section for two extra bonus money making methods.

1. Creating your Own Information Product

This includes books, courses, e-books, audio discs, videos, DVD's, etc.

Don't freak out – anyone can do this, just keep reading.

By far the most profitable simple cash machine method is to produce your own information product and list it on Clickbank, PayDotCom or any of the other affiliate marketing sites so that others (affiliates) will sell your product for you and receive a cut of the profits (commission).

You provide the product and the marketing tools and the affiliates, if the product is a good one that solves a problem, will promote and sell it for you. Simple – you do the work once then let others sell it for you, bringing you a nice monthly income!

The hardest thing, in my experience, is to decide on a subject for your product.

Have a look round the Clickbank Marketplace (www.clickbank.com) to see which products are selling well. For example, if you are interested in Self Help, check out that section on the left hand side of the page. At the time of writing, the top product in the Self Help category is "The Tao Of Badass - Dating Advice For Men" and has a *gravity of 327.41.

*The 'gravity' will give you an idea of how well the product is selling.

The gravity of a product is basically how many separate affiliates have sold the product recently, the more the better as then you know that lots of different people promoting the product in different ways are having success with it.

In my opinion, anything above 20 signifies that there are buyers in that market, but anything over 50 is much better and over 100 is a hot market! (…or a hit product, but at least you know people in that market are willing to buy products).

Could you produce a similar product?

Another way to find ideas for an information product is to go to Google.com or any search engine and type what I call 'query words' into the search bar.

For example:

How can I…

How to…

Tips for…

Advice on…

Where can I find…

Advice for…

You will see that Google shows you what other people have been searching for in a drop down box e.g.

'Advice for – the bride'

'Advice for – first time buyers'

'Tips for – running'

Top Tip: Make sure you are signed out of your Google account before you search or Google will return suggestions loosely based on your own previous searches.

Maybe you could write an ebook on 'Advice for the Bride' or 'Tips for Running' etc. Think up some of your own 'query words' to see what you can come up with.

You are looking for people who have a problem that they want solved. You will be providing the solution.

If you are not a writer it may prove difficult to create a product without investing some money for outsourcing.

But you may be able to produce a fantastic video course yourself – for free. You may know someone, a friend or relative who is a good writer and will put your ideas into words for a cut of the profits.

If you have speech to text software like Dragon Naturally Speaking, you could simply dictate your ideas and get someone to edit it to make a polished product.

Think of ways to create your product that won't require too much investment.

Once you have your product and promotional materials for your affiliates, you need to list your product on Clickbank or any other affiliate marketplace you choose. In some cases this will require paying a fee.

But, if your product is well presented, popular and sells well, you will make this initial investment back pretty quickly.

Once your fantastic product is listed and affiliates begin to promote it you can sit back and watch the money roll in.

2. Write and Self-Publish Books

Please don't disregard this, it is not as mad (or as difficult…) as it sounds.

Even if you are not a great writer you should still be able to get a book or two out there. You don't have to be Jane Austin or William Shakespeare to sell books.

As long as you provide value for your readers you should be able make a nice residual income. You don't have to write a 'War and Peace' tome; a short book with great content that helps your readers should sell well.

Do you have any hobbies or interests that you know a lot about?

You may be a wizard at graphics, know a few good cheats for a popular game or you may be very knowledgeable about stamp collecting or gardening.

Whatever your interest - write about that.

However obscure your subject there will be lots more people who share your enthusiasm or people who want to learn more about your interest.

Perhaps you have a folder of old family recipes or an unusual life story, maybe you have a strong opinion on the meaning of life or you know tons about living the student lifestyle, these ideas could make great books.

Begin by taking a sheet of paper and writing down all your interests and hobbies.

Next take some time to think about which of these you would find it easiest to write about; it will usually be the area that you enjoy most.

Now write a list of topics within that subject – these will be your chapters. Take each topic in turn and write about it as fully as you can.

Write your introduction (telling your readers what you are going to tell them) and conclusion (telling your readers what you have told them).

Now write a few paragraphs about yourself explaining who you are, how you know about the subject and how their problems will be solved if they read your book; what will they learn from you?

Put everything together in the order that you want it.

You are going to self-publish this book on Createspace.com.

You need to format your completed book for uploading to Createspace.

Remember that Createspace **will only print your book exactly as you have written it – they will not correct any mistakes.**

So check your copy – then check it again!

This is the way I format my books, there are lots of other ways but this works for me:

I use a Word doc when writing my book. On the page layout tab, choose the page size and set it to A5 with 'normal' margins. If you want a footer, add one now and, at the same time, add page numbers from the 'insert' tab.

Create a table of contents then, when everything is exactly as you want to be in your published book, turn the Word doc into a .pdf file by choosing 'save as' in the 'file' tab then choose the 'pdf option.

See below:

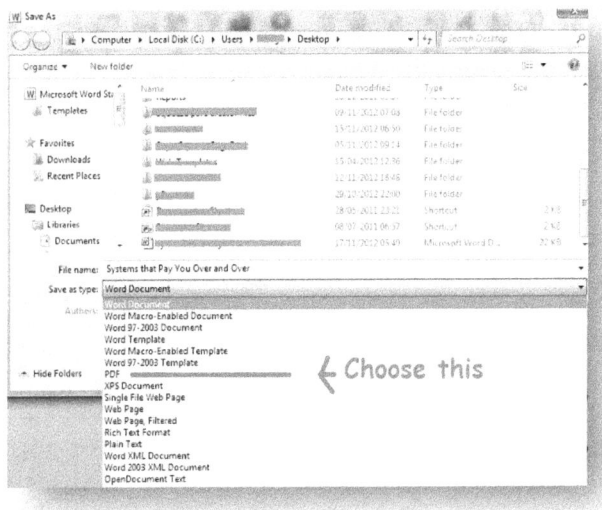

This .pdf file is what you will upload to Createspace.

Next you need a cover for your book.

You could use the free cover design that Createspace offer, it allows you to change colours, fonts, add photos and descriptions etc. or you could find a good graphic designer to do this for you.

Never use a 3D cover as you would for an ebook, always use a flat one.

Important Note: Be sure to use a bold background colour to make your book cover stand out on Amazons white background.

Have a look at the bestselling books in your genre to see the type of book covers that are being used.

Set up your free account at www.Createspace.com and follow the instructions to set up your details and your new book for publication. Then upload your files as instructed (*when you are asked for the preferred book size choose 5.25" x 8" if you have used the A5 page sizing as above*).

You then need to wait until you get an email telling you that your files have been approved.

Go back to your Createspace account and order a proof copy; it will cost around $10 including p&p.

When it arrives, check it carefully to make sure everything is exactly as you want it to be and check it for spelling and grammar errors.

If your book needs any revisions, correct it within your source file then re-save as a .pdf as above and re-upload your file to Createspace as before.

Order another proof copy to make sure that everything is fine. Once your book is exactly as you want it to be, click the 'publish' button on your Createspace book page.

That's it – you're done!

Your book will appear on Amazon's website within a day or two and will be listed for people to buy for as long as you leave it there.

It is a good idea to get some reviews for your book and do some promotion to get the sales started.

After all, if no-one knows your book is available, no-one will buy it.

There are lots of great products that will show you how to get your book noticed. There are also lots of products that will give you a more detailed description of how to upload your book to Createspace than is provided here.

Now you can either get to work on your next simple money machine book, or simply sit back and wait for your commission cheques to start coming in from the first one.

But remember the more books you self-publish in this way, the more money you will receive each month.

It is a numbers game.

I still get monthly royalties for the very first book I self-published back in 2009 without doing any more work at all.

In fact, the royalty payments from my self-published books take care of my mortgage payments each month and yours could too – eventually, if you do the initial work.

N.B. **For anyone living outside USA** – you really should get a US tax number in order to avoid Createspace withholding 30% of your royalties. It is quick and easy to do – Createspace have instructions on their site. Make this a priority so you won't lose 30% of your royalties.

3. Email Marketing using an Autoresponder

This is another easy way to make a recurring income – once you have taken the time to set everything up properly.

The first thing to do is to sign up for a good autoresponder service – I use www.GetResponse.com. They offer the first month FREE (my favourite price ☺…), then after the first month you will pay a monthly fee according the number of subscribers you have.

You will also need hosting because you are going to put up a squeeze page in order to collect email addresses.

I use Hostgator because they are very reliable and the customer service is second to none when you are just starting out.

Another necessity is a domain name. You could use your own name or a generic one that can be used for lots of things, your own name is a good example. www.GoDaddy.com is a good place to start.

Next you need to find a good information product that you can offer free in exchange for an email address.

You could write one yourself or find a good ***PLR** product for a few dollars that you can edit to make it your own. To find a PLR product in your chosen niche simply do a Google search as follows: PLR [your niche].

20

*PLR = Private Label Rights – which means you usually have permission to edit the entire product and add your own name as author of the product.

Always check the license of any product that you intend to use to make sure you have complete freedom to do as you wish with it.

Make sure that the product you are going to use as a giveaway is top quality and not some piece of illegible garbage that has been thrown together.

The product needs to be relevant to the offers that you will eventually be promoting.

So, if you intend to promote affiliate (or your own) products on Dog Training, your freebie should be something to do with dogs. Or if you intend to promote Photography products, your freebie should be something to do with photography – you get the idea…

Now it's time to set up your squeeze page with the opt-in box that you have created within your autoresponder.

You can pick up some very good free squeeze page templates by doing a Google search.

Make sure that you have a good cover for your freebie ebook or report to make it look tempting. If you are using a PLR product always have a fresh, new cover created.

You will need to set up a series of emails within your autoresponder so that the people who sign up to receive

21

your freebie will get automatic emails from you. You can either write these emails yourself or pay someone else to write them for you.

I usually start by writing 12 emails with **about 5 of these containing either a link to my own product or a link to a good product that I am an affiliate for** – this is how you will make money. (Note: I never promote a product that I have not bought and tried myself).

Next load these into your autoresponder to be delivered at predetermined intervals. I send one every week on the same day. If you are not sure how to set this up there are lots of excellent tutorials on GetResponse or on YouTube.

You have now finished setting up your simple money making machine which should result in quite a few monthly sales as long as you have built a good relationship with your subscribers. You will need to add more emails to your autoresponder periodically in order to keep the money coming in.

If you find a good product that you think will interest your subscribers, you can send a 'one-off' email to inform them of the product.

The only thing you need to do now is to get traffic to get people to subscribe to your list. There are lots of information products that teach you how to get traffic, both free and paid, to your squeeze page.

4. Set up a Zazzle Store

Zazzle is a site that provides lots of products that customers can choose then add an image to customise it. You provide the images for people to add to the products.

Zazzle says, *"Zazzle is the world's leading platform for quality custom products. Zazzle's proprietary technology enables individuals, professional artists, and major brands, including Harry Potter and Hallmark, to create and offer billions of unique products for customers worldwide. Zazzle's rapidly expanding product base covers every topic imaginable and includes t-shirts, business cards, invitations, in addition to a variety of custom gifts. Upon creation, products are instantly and accurately visualized on the site and offered in the Zazzle marketplace. When ordered, each product is made on-demand, typically within 24 hours. Launched in 2005 and based in Redwood City, California."*

Zazzle is a print on demand (POD) site which allows users to buy as customers or sell as store owners.

They accept all the major credit cards, PayPal and Zazzle Gift Vouchers and operate worldwide.

Zazzle allows you to create and promote products at no cost to you.

You get paid when people buy your products and also when you send people to Zazzle who buy products from other sellers – in the same way Amazon and other affiliate systems work.

It doesn't cost you anything beyond your time and creativity to start making money.

Zazzle take care of the manufacturing, inventory, shipping, and customer service, leaving you free to concentrate on designing and promoting the products you want to sell virtually.

You don't have to retain a stock of products to be in business. You simply upload a digital image made with software like Photoshop, GIMP or any image editing software.

You then 'create' products using the blank templates supplied by Zazzle.

Zazzle has a base cost for each "blank" template item in their inventory. When you add your own design to an item you get to choose what percentage royalty you want from the sale.

You may earn royalties from your own products or referral (affiliate) fees from sales of other Zazzlers' products.

Like Amazon, Zazzle has cookies that mean you get sales from other stores on their site if the visitor follows a referral link of your making.

You can even earn referral fees for your own products.

There are full instructions on the site showing you how to go about setting up your new store.

To sign up for an account and set up your own store go to www.zazzle.co.uk/sell and follow the very simple instructions.

5. Kindle Books

A lot of the information for publishing Kindle Books also applies to books that you may write for self-publishing with Createspace. In fact, you can publish any of your books with both Createspace and Kindle; you would just have to adjust the formatting to suit each publishing platform.

Under the Amazon Kindle Direct Publishing program, anyone with a great story or content to share can effortlessly create their very own books to sell on Amazon Kindle, earning up to 70% royalties along the way.

Contrary to what you may think, this is a very easy process. Not only that, there is no limit to the subject matter, which means that you can publish lots of books on various topics in order to maximize your earnings. You could publish fiction or non-fiction but for the purposes of this book, we will concentrate on non-fiction.

Consider this; what if you publish one book and you get around 30 sales @ .99c per month with a royalty of just 30%. That's nearly $10 per book. Now imagine if you increase your offering to several books – say 10-20. But don't forget, you will get 75% royalty on any books that are priced between $2.99 and $9.99. You do the math…

Not only are there no additional fees and considering that digital books are a one-time investment, meaning you only have to create a digital book once, you could quickly recover any initial investment such as the cover design, editing and even the outsourcing of the writing and make a very nice recurring profit as well.

If you intend to publish books in a few different genres, you could use pen names to keep the subjects separate. This helps to establish you as 'expert' in a particular genre.

Kindle publishing is very easy when compared to the real-world hassles of having to sell your manuscript to publishing houses or persuading publishing agents sign you up as one of their authors.

In fact, it is so easy almost anyone can do it.

Publishing your Non-Fiction Work on Amazon Kindle

Before beginning to write your book, the very first decision to make would be the topic you want to write about. You may want to publish a book on your favourite hobby or your own Family Recipe Book, or you may have lots of other ideas.

When trying to figure out what to write about, you could consider the seasons. For example, a month or two before the holiday seasons, it would be good to write about any of the following:

Christmas

- Gift Buying Tips

- Decorating Tips

- Holiday Do-it-Yourself Guides (such as DIY Christmas gifts, DIY Christmas Decors)

- Dishes to Serve on Christmas Eve

- Baking ideas for Christmas.

New Year

- How to Celebrate the New Year

- New Year Gift-Giving

- Crafts

- Party Ideas

- New Year Resolutions

Valentines Day

- Dating Tips

- Romantic Baking Ideas

- Top Dating Restaurants (in the form of a review)

- Dishes to serve

- Romantic gift Ideas

Halloween

- Original Costume ideas

- Spooky Party Food

- Party Themes

As you may know, demand for reading resources usually increases just before a particular season but there are many other topics that you can write about whatever the season.

Sex and Relationships, Health and Well-being, Yoga, Meditation, Food, Self Help topics, Diet and even Technology are just a few of the more popular subjects.

Another great way to get some inspiration is to check Amazon's Bestseller's list.

Writing an Information or 'How to' book

Once you have decided on a topic it's time to get some writing done. Below is my blueprint for writing an information book in the shortest time possible.

An age-old proven format for writing any information based book is:

1. Tell them what you are going to tell them (*Introduction*)

2. Tell them (*Body of book*)

3. Tell them what you have told them (C*onclusion*)

The Title

Choose something that is interesting and catches the eye. In most cases it is the title and book cover that sells the book to a prospective purchaser.

If you are writing about Training your Dog, try using something like:

"15 Simple Secrets for Training your Dog

Every Frustrated Dog Owner Should Know"

or

"The Idiots Guide to Training your Idiot Dog"

(I'm going to use that one for my next Dog book!)

Your reader will be more likely to check out your book if the title promises something different, **so be creative**.

Remember to include the keywords in the title (the words that people may type into the Amazon search bar when looking for a book – in this case, Training your Dog).

Introduction

Write the introduction to your book. Use three or four paragraphs outlining what the book is about and why they need to read it.

In the introduction always remember to tell your prospective reader exactly how the book will help them and what benefits they are likely to get from your book.

They are not interested in why you wrote the book, your inspiration nor your past history. They are only interested in "What's in it For Me" - so make sure your introduction tells them.

Body

Write down a ***list of relevant topics*** you want to cover in your book – these will become your chapter titles.

Begin the list with the first topic that you will write about and then progress *logically* through to the conclusion. You can always change stuff around later if you need to.

Now take each topic and write a few paragraphs about it. Six or seven hundred words for each topic is about right but that is up to you – whatever it takes to explain the subject fully.

Conclusion

Write your conclusion and reiterate exactly what the reader has learned.

Add the legal stuff; copyright and disclaimers to your book. You could also add a little about you – the author.

The final step is to proofread and edit your book. My advice is to do this once when you have finished it; then put it away for at least three days.

Proofread and edit one more time – it's amazing the small mistakes you can find that you missed the first time round.

Remember, even a low priced digital book should be your very best work.

There you have it, a simple step-by-step method to writing any information based book.

It doesn't have to be a War and Peace tome; it can be whatever length it takes to get the information across to your readers.

Top Tip: As Amazon have a 'look inside' feature which will show a potential purchaser around 10% of your book as a preview, it is a good idea to make sure that the first part of your book contains a lot of teaser content. The main points should be kept for later in the book – after the browser has purchased.

Designing the Cover for Your Book

One of the things that can help sales when releasing your book would be the cover.

For a digital product, the customer doesn't really see much of the product. So, it is important that you convince your customer not only with the content but with how the product looks – in this case, the book cover.

To help in designing your book cover, I have prepared a short list of things to consider that could help increase your conversion rates.

Be clear about what the book is all about. Whilst design is a very important part of the book, you should also remember that your customers are looking for information – and they have to know that the information they are looking for will be found in your book.

Don't forget to include the name (or pen name) of the author. This may not exactly be much help to the new Kindle publisher.

However once you have created a name for yourself in the business, having your name appear on the cover would help increase the book's authority which in turn, would increase sales.

Even if you're a new writer, this can also be an advantage to you – it could even be the first step to creating a name for yourself within your chosen genre (branding).

Use a Bold Color. Amazons pages are white, so use a color for your cover that will stand out. I made the mistake of using pastel covers for my first few books until I realized that a bold color attracts more attention.

Use a Flat Cover – not a 3D cover that you would use for an ebook. Check out how best-selling authors design their covers for Amazon.

Formatting and Uploading your Book to Kindle

Save your book file in the correct format.

When using Word to write your book, make sure that you choose the A5 page size and set all your margins to 1.00. A couple of other things to take note of when you're preparing your material for Kindle:

- The best fonts to use are the simple ones. I use Verdana 12pt and 1.15 line spacing for all my Kindle books.

- The simpler the format, the better it is. People reading on their Kindles or other devices for that matter, are looking for great content not jazzy design. Save the creative design for your cover.

- If you need a page break, **insert it manually** through the Word toolbar. If you just hit return Kindle leaves a white space rather than starting a new page as you intended.

- Allow your text to run on through your pages as you type. Remember this is digital publishing, so the rules are different than publishing physical books.

- It is also is worth mentioning that people who will buy your digital books will be reading your content on devices no bigger than half the size of your laptop's screen. So, bear that in mind when formatting your book.

- If you're planning to wrap text around an image, you may want to check whether or not the text has actually wrapped around the image – or if it has been bumped to the next page (personally, I never wrap text around a picture – it saves hassle).

- **Don't** use a header, footer or page numbers for Kindle publishing.

Save a copy of your book to your desktop so you still have a copy of the source file, then open the copy and go to 'File' then 'save as'.

Save the file as 'Webpage, filtered' as below:

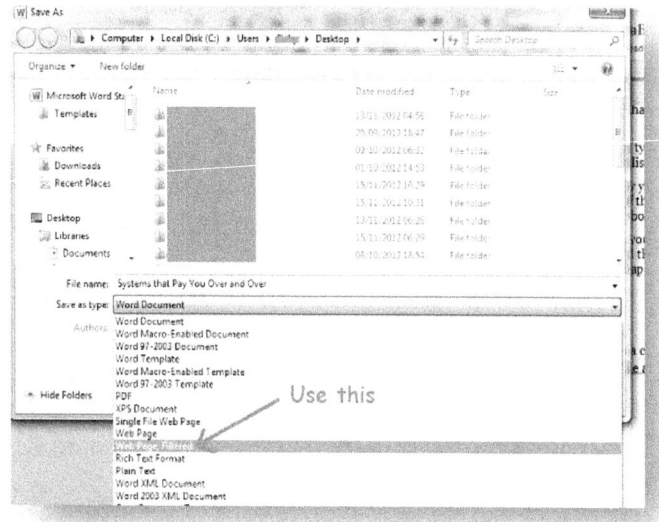

5 Simple Money Machine Series   ©L J Samuels

IMPORTANT

If your book contains images you will see that when you have saved your file as 'Webpage filtered' two sections appear on your desktop. One is a folder containing all your images; the other is the filtered webpage. In order to make your images show up when viewed on the Kindle reader you should:

1. Create a new folder on your desktop and move the two folders to the new folder. It doesn't work if you simply add your filtered webpage to the picture folder.

2. Give the new folder a name then save to a .zip file.

The .zip file is the one that you will upload to Kindle.

Download the free ebook reader so you can check out how your book will appear on a Kindle. If the book doesn't appear as you would like it to, make notes so you remember what to change.

You can make the necessary changes before uploading it to your Kindle 'Bookshelf'.

Register with Amazon's Kindle Direct Publishing

Next go to www.Amazon.com and scroll to the bottom of the home page. See below:

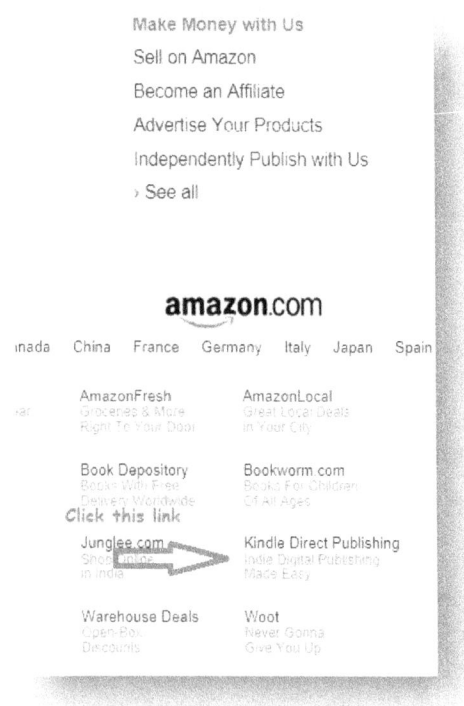

Before you can start uploading book files you have to create your account. Follow the simple onscreen instructions. After agreeing to the terms, you will be required to enter additional information such as Name, Address, Country and the option by which you opt to receive your royalties.

Once you've filled out the form, click on the save button at the bottom right of the page.

Amazon will save your information and you will be notified with "**Your account information has been successfully saved**".

Next, click on "BOOKSHELF" at the top of the page.

Uploading your Digital Book

Remember: Before you upload your first book, download the free Kindle Previewer so you can check out how your book will appear on the Kindle. You will find this next to the 'upload file' option. If the book doesn't appear as you would like it to, you can make the changes before uploading it to your 'Bookshelf'

Now it's time to actually upload your book. On the Bookshelf, click "ADD NEW TITLE".

There are tooltips provided for almost every field. If you are uncertain about what they are for, click on the fields respective "WHAT'S THIS?" link and the further explanation will be provided.

In the 'description' field provide a full description of your book and how it can help the reader solve their problem. **This is your sales copy – make it good.**

Choose two relevant categories for your book and use all seven keywords (tags) that you are allowed.

At the bottom of the page, you will be required to upload your book file (the .zip file you created earlier) and Amazon will convert it to Kindle format automatically. Please be patient as upload time depends on the size of your book file and your internet speed.

You will be taken to the next step of the process where you will be required to enter additional information. This will be the last step before your digital book will be published

When setting the price for your book, remember that 70% royalties are only available if your book is between $2.99 and $9.99. The royalty is 30% for any other price point.

Check the box to add your book to Kindle Book Lending. You will get paid each time someone borrows your book.

After you have satisfactorily completed the information required, you will be returned to the 'bookshelf' with your book in the queue.

I strongly recommend that you enroll your book in Kindle Select - you will find details on your 'Bookshelf' page.

Note: Your book will say "in review" as its status. As a policy, Amazon reviews all content submitted to them. English content takes up to 24 hours, with Amazon's effort to strengthen the Kindle experience and ensure high quality among all its products.

If you would like to read more about this, you may click the "What's this?" link under the status on the page.

You can change the price, title and description of your books at any time. Just edit the fields required and click 'save'.

Don't delete the book and republish it as you will lose any ranking that the book may have achieved. It will still go into the 'in review' status but you keep any rankings your book may have achieved.

Marketing your Book

It is no good simply writing and uploading your book to Kindle then sitting and waiting for the sales to flood in – it won't happen.

You may be lucky and get quite a few sales but, if you want your book to be listed on Amazon's bestsellers list you have to do some promotion.

Marketing your book is outside the scope of this book so head over to Amazon and join some of the Kindle communities. There is lots of useful information available there.

Bonus Money Making Method 1

First I want you to think about the paragraph below:

If someone is running full speed at you, is it easier to stand your ground and try to stop them when they run into you or get behind them and push them forward?

Since they're already moving forward, it only makes sense that you'd have an easier and less painful time pushing them in the direction they're already headed in.

I'll give you just one example and this will tell you everything you need to know about how to make some 'Easy Money'. Just use your imagination to take this further.

Let's say you start getting a lot of emails promoting one new product or product launch in particular and this product seems to have a lot of buzz (negative or positive it doesn't matter) and affiliates behind it.

Many people I speak to tell me they simply delete emails like that (because they see those emails as being annoying) and all I can do is smile to myself because I know what emails like that really are - easy money.

Remember what I said about how it is better to help people move in the direction they're already headed in? Well, if people have their minds completely made up to promote a particular product then why not help them find more ways to do it?

Provide the shovels.

For example, you could create (or hire someone to create) a simple series of 5-7 articles promoting that product and then sell the reprint rights to your email series at $10-20 a pop.

Sell just 50 copies of your email series and you've made $500-$1,000 for something that should only take you a day or two in setup time.

You don't have to worry about researching a niche, creating a huge product, managing affiliates, setting up joint ventures or any of that.

And, you can set it all up so that Paypal.com pays you immediately whenever you make a sale because instant cash is always great.

The best part is that you don't have to find out if there's a demand for your information because you can clearly see that there is, just from the sheer number of places you see promoting the product you're going to create an email series to endorse.

Don't forget to collect the email addresses of your purchasers so you can contact them with your next email series.

I send an email with a link to a simple sales page where my clients can purchase the email series instantly.

Add a Paypal button so you get paid right away.

Use your imagination to think of other ways you can 'supply the shovels'.

Everyone wants an easier way to do something they are already doing. You just have to think of ways to supply the solution.

The beauty of this idea is that you can do it several times a month and every time you do, you add to your list of people who will look forward to the next email series you create.

In fact, I have people email me to ask me to create an email series for an upcoming launch.

I will create an email series to order but I never create a series exclusively for just one person.

Why would I want to make $100 by creating a series for just one person when I can sell the same work to 50-100 people @ $10+ each?

Any series I create is available (for a fee...) to anyone who wants to promote the product featured in the email series.

Bonus Money Making Method 2

Do you enjoy photography?

You could make a nice chunk of change by signing up to one of the digital photography sites and uploading your photos.

As with the other money making methods in this book, it will take time to build your reputation but if you offer good quality, interesting or unusual photographs, in time you will make money.

There are tons of people (like me...) who need images for their websites, books, reports etc. Why not sign up for a few of the sites that supply royalty free photographs, upload your images and get paid every time someone downloads your images.

A lot of the stock photography sites are very particular about the photograph quality so read the instructions for each site very carefully to find out the requirements for size, minimum quality etc.

The subject matter on these sites is endless; from the common, everyday situation to the strange and outlandish – it's all there.

So if you take photos of animals, cars, people in any situation, gorillas sleeping, ants building a cottage or just landscapes – someone is looking for that type of image for a project.

Do a Google search for royalty free photo sites and follow the instructions to sign up and get paid for your hobby – there's nothing better than that!

My final thoughts (in this section):

The main reason for setting up a few of these simple money making machines is to avoid 'having all your eggs in the same basket'.

If you only had one source of income, perhaps a blog that is making lots of money via adsense, advertising, affiliate marketing etc., just imagine how disastrous it would be if the rules changed and you could no longer make money with that blog – for whatever reason.

Your income would dry up very quickly.

So it makes a lot of sense to add additional streams of income that will continue to send you money for a long time – whatever happens.

As I said at the beginning of this book, nothing will be achieved if you simply read this book and do nothing.

Your own efforts will determine your results – create your own success because you are the only person that can.

Make a pledge to yourself to do the work to set up just one of these simple money machines in the coming week. **Then do it!**

Take Action Now!

Section TWO

5 More Simple Money Machines that Pay You Over and Over – For Very Little Work

In this section you will learn 5 more Simple Money Machines methods that will make you money *but* you will be required to do some work on a daily basis to get the best results.

"OMG, shock, horror – yet MORE WORK", I hear you say again, "This time he wants me to do some WORK each day!"

But, as I said in Section One of this book, think about it as speculating to accumulate.

The work required to implement these systems is simple, quick and even a person with only a basic understanding of internet marketing could begin to make money online with a bit of time and effort.

This time we will be putting together a few income streams that you will have to apply a little effort to in order to earn money.

1. Write a Simple Ebook and Give it away for FREE

This is not as mad as it may sound.

The idea is to write (or have written for you), a short ebook that solves a common problem, 10 to 15 pages should be enough. This problem should be related to a product, either digital or physical, that you can be an affiliate for.

Once you have the book written, add relevant affiliate links then give it away in as many places as possible.

But I'm getting ahead of myself; below is what you need to do to get the best possible results.

First you should decide on a group of products you want to promote as an affiliate. Health and Fitness is always a good one as is Internet Marketing. You could also try the ever popular Weight Loss niche.

You could be an affiliate for higher priced fitness products from Amazon like a Treadmill (at the time of writing there is one selling at $999), interesting and helpful products for the older person like a Pink Walking Stick (priced at $44.99) or one of the many weight loss digital products on Clickbank Primal Burn which pays around $42 per sale.

If you decide to go for digital (downloadable) products and don't like the idea of waiting for your commission payments, you may want to sign up for Rapbank – it's free.

There are hundreds of products to promote and the beauty of this site is that you get paid directly to your Paypal account *immediately*. No waiting a few months for your money – that has got to be good!

We are looking for a product in a niche where people are proven to spend money solving a problem. People who play golf are usually obsessive about their hobby and will spend money to improve their techniques. There are also a lot of people who are new to the game and are searching for tips on the rules etc.

I have chosen a product from Rapbank.com that has golf training videos. It sells for $47 with a commission of 50%.

After reading the sales page I learn that this product seems to be for people who are new to the game and are lacking in confidence.

So, I will write a short ebook about how to be a confident person or what sort of equipment is needed to begin playing golf or even a book about self-belief when playing your first round of golf.

You get the idea – make your book relevant to the product or group of products that you are going to promote.

Add your cloaked affiliate link to the digital product that you are promoting.

For instance, I would say something like, **"If you are ready to learn so much more about [*your subject*], CLICK HERE for a great, comprehensive product that will make things much easier for you to [*whatever it is that you are talking about*]."**

When writing your book you could add one or two links to other products that are available in your chosen niche, but don't go overboard. No-one wants to read a book that is all affiliate links.

In the golf example I could go on to add one or two affiliate links to Amazons golf products or sign up to be an affiliate to a golf site that sells equipment.

Add a paragraph both at the beginning and the end of the book encouraging the reader to share the book with their friends on Facebook, Twitter and anywhere they choose.

At the very end of your book add a Resource Page where you can again add the clickable links to the main product and any ancillary products that you are promoting.

Create a squeeze page requiring people to add their email address in order to get your free book.

You then have a list of people to market to with other products in that niche.

Next you should get a good, eye-catching book cover created.

5 Simple Money Machine Series ©L J Samuels

You could have someone from Fiverr.com create one for you but make sure you do some research into the people who offer that service. Some are brilliant whilst others are absolute rubbish. I know it's only $5 but you still want to get the best possible cover that you can.

Please make the book worth reading – no-one will share it or click on your links if the book is badly written with poor spelling and grammar or is simply filled with links and does not have any actionable content. Make it your very best work.

Set up a simple download page for your free book and upload the book to your server.

On the download page beneath the download link to your free book add a headline that says something like:

"Wait, Here's Something Fantastic That May Help You With [the problem]"

Then add the banner or a simple link to the product that you are promoting as an affiliate in the book or better still, your own product.

Now we need to get some exposure for the book.

Ask your friends to share the link to your squeeze page on twitter and Facebook – remember, it's free so you should get quite a few downloads.

Join some of the forums relating to your book. You can find plenty through a search. Simply type "[your niche] + forum" (without quote marks) and see what comes up.

Visit a few each day and, if the forum seems very active, join up and begin to add comments.

After a while (as determined by each individual forum) you will be able to add a signature link leading to your free download page. Use the word 'FREE' in your anchor text.

Always aim to add something to the discussion.

Make sure your comments are relevant and avoid one-liners such as "great post" – forum members hate that and will ignore your nicely crafted signature link.

Spend about an hour a day joining forums and commenting so your link is exposed to as many people as possible.

Another place to add your free book is to some of the free file hosting upload sites.

Another site to list your book is www.tradebit.com. List it for 1 cent.

Advertise your free book on Craigslist – everyone likes free stuff.

If you are promoting something in the internet marketing niche, join the Warrior Forum. It has hundreds of thousands of active members and you can add a clickable signature link.

Again, there are lots of other internet marketing forums but Warrior Forum is one of the most active out there.

You could make a short but interesting video relating to your free book for YouTube, putting the link to your free book in the first line of the description. Remember to use keywords for the title. Keywords are words that people will type into the search bar when they are looking for something on YouTube.

Finally, think of as many places you can to distribute your free ebook and very soon you should begin to see money coming in as people buy through the links in your free book. Also, the bonus of using this method is that you are building a list that you can market to later.

This method takes a while to set up but, if your book is informative, well written, and you spend time each day adding your free book to places where people can see and download it, you should make money.

2. Craigslist Method One

Unless you have been living under the proverbial rock you will have heard of Craigslist. This is the site we will be making use of for this method.

We will become the 'middleman' for those who are looking for a service on Craigslist. Although this takes a while to set up, once you get the hang of it, you will be able to find lots of 'gigs' and match them up with providers.

Go to Craigslist.com and, on the bottom right of the page you will see a section named 'gigs' as shown below.

The next step is to check out these 'gigs' to see what people are looking for. For example, the 'writing' section gave me these results:

Bilingual Spanish-English Interpreter Needed - (Atlanta Metro)

Bilingual Vietnamese-English Interpreter Needed - (Atlanta Metro)

Call for Writers...Fantasy, Science Fiction - (Atlanta and Nationwide)

Lifestyle Blog - Guest Writers - (Everywhere)

Write my essay -

Assistant/ Intern Wanted - (Cobb County)

Typist needed - (Smyrna)

writers interns wanted - (ATL)

Sports Fans needed (College sports too!) - 123ST -

Looking for blogger to help Cosplay/Anime/Manga site - (Atlanta)

Looking for editors! - (Anywhere!)

Sponsorship Cordinator - (Internet)

Next you need to see which of these gigs are paid.

Some will be people wanting you to work for free; obviously we are not interested in these.

But there are lots of people that are offering paid work. Below is one that we could use:

Reply 5lx57-361506518ⱺgigs.craigslist.org   flag : miscategorized prohibited spam best of

Writer Needed for Content Re-writing (Atlanta)

Local independent web developer needs a content rewriter for projects. Multiple projects weekly.

- Location: Atlanta
- it's NOT ok to contact this poster with services or other commercial interests
- Compensation depends on the projetct

Once you have found a decent gig that offers payment it's time to contact the advertiser and offer your services.

Don't panic – you won't need to do his content re-writing, we will be finding someone else to do that.

Once you have been awarded the job you need to find someone to do the job.

Head over to www.fiverr.com and search for 'rewriting'.

Here are the results I got:

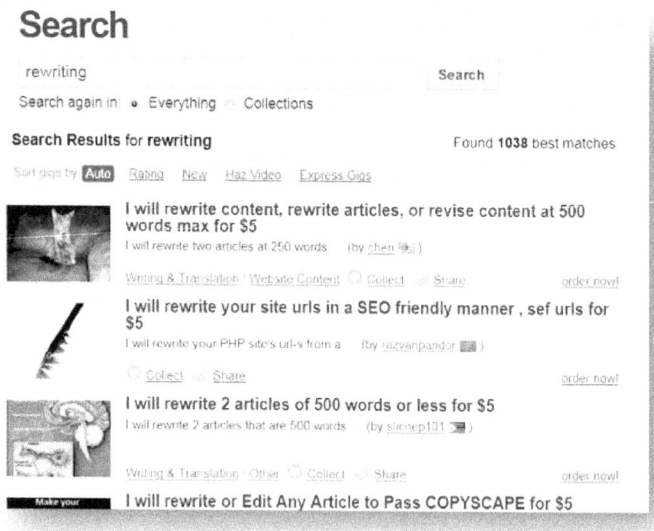

As you can see from the image above there were 1038 matches for this search. So there are plenty of people to do the work.

You will need to do your research to find a well recommended person to do your job.

That's it – you land a gig on Craigslist that pays more than $10 and get the job done by someone on Fiverr for $5.

You can do this over and over and make a nice chunk of change to put towards a holiday, a treat for the family etc.

The only requirement for this method is to be organized and spend time doing your research.

Another way to utilize Craiglist classified ads is to sell a service – don't worry we'll be getting the work done on Fiverr.

We'll be doing the opposite of the first Craigslist Method; we'll be **advertising our services** then finding someone to do the work *after* we have secured the job.

This is quick and easy.

First write a good advertisement or find someone who will write one for you.

As it is free to advertise on Craigslist, you can offer as many services as you like because you won't be doing any of the work.

You can offer web design, writing services, graphics, video, voice-over etc, etc,.

Once you begin to get enquiries head over to Fiverr and find someone who is offering the service you require and purchase a 'gig'.

When you are negotiating a job, never promise anything you can't deliver. If you think it will take 5 days to deliver a job, tell your client it will take 8 days so, when you deliver the work in 6 days, he will be delighted with the fast turnaround.

Delivering work late is a big no-no and will result in bad feeling and no repeat business.

Try and give the client something extra. For example, if you are writing a few articles for him, search out some good PLR articles on the same topic and do a quick rewrite and send him those as a free bonus. Be sure to tell him that they are PLR re-writes.

If you are providing graphics add extra free.

Become the person who provides value for money.

This is actually a very profitable method. For example you can charge $15 per article and get it written for $5, or you can charge $25 for designing a book cover and get it done for $5.

Remember to collect email addresses for the future.

If I need some extra money for a project I simply email past clients and tell them that I am offering a special deal 'for two days only' – I always get some work.

Again, you need to be organized and present a very professional persona to your prospective clients so you will be the 'go-to' person for everything they need doing.

I no longer have time to advertise on Craigslist but still get emails from clients I found using this method.

3 Craiglist – Method 2

This method involves using the forum on Craiglist – no advertising or answering adverts.

If you don't have a Craigslist account – sign up now. No need for phone verification to use the forums.

Once you have created your forum username you will have to wait a week before you can post clickable links.

Now head over to the forums www.forums.craigslist.org

You will find a list of all the different forum subjects.

Find a good product that you are an affiliate for and get the link.

5 Simple Money Machine Series   ©L J Samuels

Use one of the many URL shorteners to disguise the fact that you are promoting an affiliate product.

If you have your own product, link to your squeeze page.

Have a look through the forum categories to find the one that best matches your product.

Write a title for your new thread – make it eye-catching without being salesy.

When you start the thread don't put your link in the first post. For example, if you are promoting a health product use the 'health & healing' category.

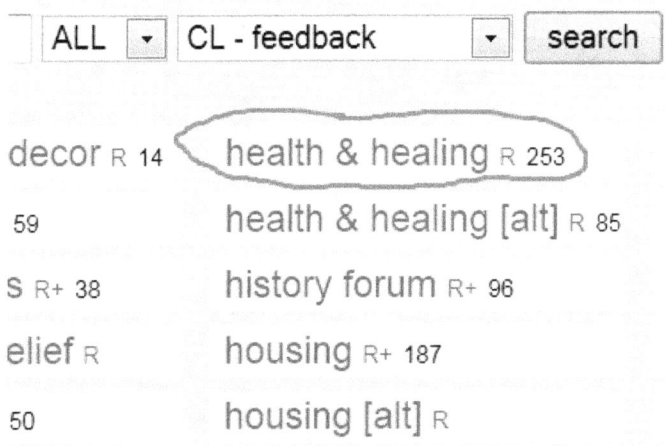

The first post should be asking if anyone has a solution to the problem that you are going to solve in your next post.

Once you get an answer, you can add another comment saying something like,

"Thanks for your suggestions, I'll check it out. I have found another great solution at [your link]."

You can do this as many times as you like in as many categories as you like.

You could try promoting in the first post like a few others seem to do but I have found that the 'softly, softly' approach works best.

You can also use the craigslist forum method to direct traffic to your website.

This method really does work best if you add a few interesting posts now and again to get yourself established as an expert.

4. YouTube

For this method we will choose a product to promote that pays directly to our Paypal account as soon as you make a sale.

There are quite a few affiliate network to choose from – Rapbank, Digiresults, Click2sell, Paydotcom etc. Some of these are instant payment, others pay weekly.

Browse these sites and find a product that you want to promote. Be sure that the product sales page is appealing; one that would convince *you* to buy. There are some really crappy sales pages around and if it doesn't look convincing to you, why would it to anyone else?

It is also a good sign that the product is well thought out and professional if the product owner provides affiliate tools for you to use.

Choose some images from the sales page or from the affiliate promotional material to use when you make your video. Choose some text that explains what the product will do for the purchaser.

Remember, everyone wants to know…

'What's in it for me?'

If you are already familiar with creating and uploading a video, that's great. Use the material that you have taken from the product information and create a simple slide

65

show. Add some background music and you're done. But if you are not familiar with video creation there are two methods to achieve the same end.

1. Go to www.Animoto.com where you can make a simple 30 second video for free. Animoto is very simple to use, simply follow the step-by-step instructions and you will have a free 30 second video to use.

2. Or you could have someone from Fiverr do it for you for $5. In my opinion, this is the better option as the guys on Fiverr are usually very good at what they do.

Right now you have your video ready to upload to YouTube.

I would recommend you create a new account for your affiliate videos using a good keyword as your channel name. See example below:

Note the number of views this video has.

This person is called 'howtomakemoneyfast12' and the video has 'howtomakemoneyfast' in the title. So when someone searches for 'how to make money fast' in the

5 Simple Money Machine Series ©L J Samuels

YouTube browser, guess what comes up in the suggestion list?

Upload your video to your new channel.

When writing your description be sure to add your cloaked affiliate link on the very first line like this:

'To get more information click the link [your link].'

(Note: remember to add http:// to your link to make it clickable. You would be surprised how many people don't do this...)

Then go on to tell your readers exactly how the product will benefit them using your keyword at least once in each paragraph.

Choose some good keywords to add in the 'keyword' field.

Now we need to get some backlinks for your video.

Head over to Fiverr again and buy a couple of 'backlink' gigs with lots of 'likes' and give them your YouTube URL.

Next you can upload your video to some of the video sharing sites. Below are a few to get you started – but there are lots more...

www.jumpcut.com

www.ourmedia.org

www.vimeo.com

www.vsocial.com

www.tremormedia.com

www.imageshack.us

www.yfrog.com

www.viddler.com

Now it's time to get your video URL out there.

If you have friends with a lot of friends on Facebook, ask them to share your video.

As in method one, join forums relating to your chosen niche, contribute to the forum then, when forum rules allow, add your video link in your signature.

Create a document in sales page format with a clickable link to your video, turn into a .pdf file then upload to document sharing sites. Do a search to find a list of these or you can email me and I will send you a long list.

Repeat the process adding more videos in the same niche to your new channel.

Spend an hour each day doing something to promote your videos; forum commenting, sharing on Facebook, uploading to more video sharing sites etc.

If you follow this plan, you will soon begin to see sales.

5. Writing for Money

There are lots of ways to earn money from writing.

We will begin with a method where you need to be able to write good, well-structured articles.

For this method we will use the site below.

www.Constant-Content.com

Constant Content is a site that allows you to write articles, upload them to your account on the site and sell them from there. They also allow users to post requests for articles where the writers bid for the work.

The first thing to point out about Constant Content is they are very rigorous in their acceptance procedure. You have to provide sample articles which are reviewed for content, spelling, grammar and punctuation. If your writing is not of an acceptable standard, you will not be accepted.

But it is well worth polishing up on any areas where you are lacking to get accepted because Constant Content can be very lucrative.

On the day I checked out the home page for this book, these are just some of the articles offered for sale.

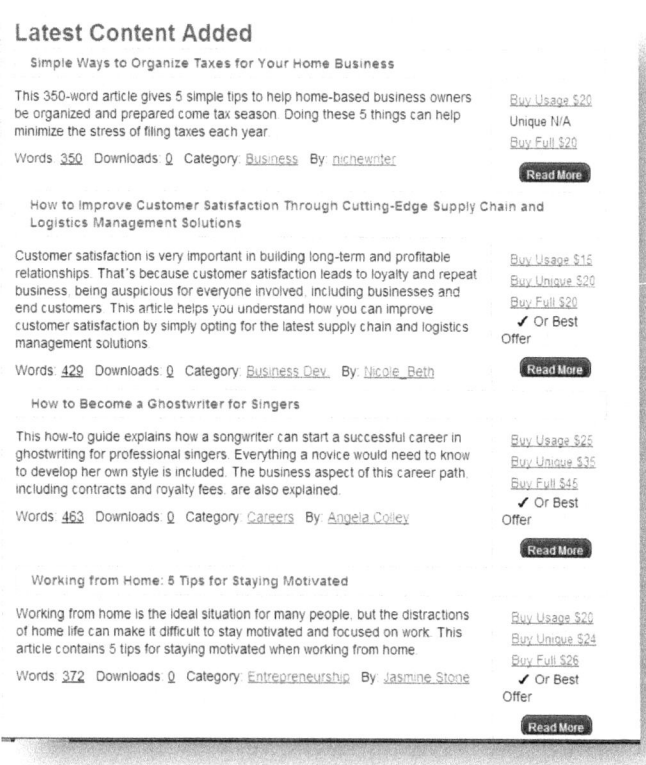

Latest Content Added

Simple Ways to Organize Taxes for Your Home Business

This 350-word article gives 5 simple tips to help home-based business owners be organized and prepared come tax season. Doing these 5 things can help minimize the stress of filing taxes each year.

Words: 350 Downloads: 0 Category: Business By: nichewriter

Buy Usage $20
Unique N/A
Buy Full $20

[Read More]

How to Improve Customer Satisfaction Through Cutting-Edge Supply Chain and Logistics Management Solutions

Customer satisfaction is very important in building long-term and profitable relationships. That's because customer satisfaction leads to loyalty and repeat business, being auspicious for everyone involved, including businesses and end customers. This article helps you understand how you can improve customer satisfaction by simply opting for the latest supply chain and logistics management solutions.

Words: 429 Downloads: 0 Category: Business Dev. By: Nicole_Beth

Buy Usage $15
Buy Unique $20
Buy Full $20
✓ Or Best Offer

[Read More]

How to Become a Ghostwriter for Singers

This how-to guide explains how a songwriter can start a successful career in ghostwriting for professional singers. Everything a novice would need to know to develop her own style is included. The business aspect of this career path, including contracts and royalty fees, are also explained.

Words: 463 Downloads: 0 Category: Careers By: Angela Colley

Buy Usage $25
Buy Unique $35
Buy Full $45
✓ Or Best Offer

[Read More]

Working from Home: 5 Tips for Staying Motivated

Working from home is the ideal situation for many people, but the distractions of home life can make it difficult to stay motivated and focused on work. This article contains 5 tips for staying motivated when working from home.

Words: 372 Downloads: 0 Category: Entrepreneurship By: Jasmine Stone

Buy Usage $20
Buy Unique $24
Buy Full $26
✓ Or Best Offer

[Read More]

You can see from the image above that there are three ways to sell your work.

1. The client can simply buy 'usage', meaning they only have the right to use the article one time. This is usually the cheapest option.

2. The client can buy 'unique' rights, which grants exclusive rights to the article. However, the content may not be altered in any way.

3. The client can buy 'full rights', meaning the client gets exclusive rights to the article – and full rights to do anything you want with it. This is the only option where the purchaser is allowed to remove the authors byline.

Once you have been accepted into Constant Content as a writer you have the ability to earn much more per article than you would elsewhere.

See below:

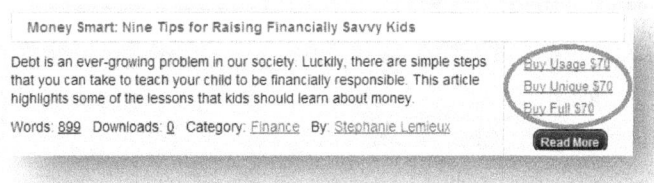

You can see from the image that this writer is charging $70 for each option. However, once he has sold either the 'unique' or 'usage' option, obviously the 'full rights' option will no longer be available. So, the aim of this is to encourage a client to buy the full rights option.

The next site that allows you to sell your articles is:

www.textbroker.com

This is much the same as constant content but the prices you can realize for your articles are not as grand.

Below is a list of other sites that pay for your writing talent.

www.associatedcontent.com

www2.brighthub.com

www.demandstudios.com

www.sponsoredreviews.com

www.triond.com

www.wisegeek.com/freelance-writing-jobs.htm

Check them out and see which ones you can make use of. All of them pay – some even pay you for the sample articles you are obliged to submit before you are accepted as a writer.

Use your writing talent to make you some extra cash.

Bonus Method

Expert Interviews

Interviewing people who are experts in their field and packaging it as your own product is one of the fastest ways to not only make money online but also to make a name for yourself in a new market.

If you create a product where you are interviewing five experts in the market and your name is attached to that product you are perceived to have a bit of authority and people will be much more inclined to spend money with you.

This simple money making strategy is extremely useful because it allows you to interact with the experts in your niche and it also gives you experience in producing your own products.

A great place to start looking for potential interviewees would be a high traffic forum where you can quickly see who are the influential players in your chosen niche.

Once you have decided on your first interviewee I suggest you send them an e-mail asking if they would be agreeable to being interviewed.

Most people are flattered to be asked and readily agree but here are some who are not interested.

If you get a 'no', simply move on to the next person – don't take it personally.

There are three ways you can conduct an interview.

1. email

2. Telephone

3. Skype

Once you and your prospective interviewee have decided which method will work best for you both, put together a list of between 20 and 30 good questions that you think are relevant and will interest your audience.

If you have decided on an e-mail interview simply send the list of questions to your subject and await the reply. Whatever method of interview you decide on, it is still a good idea to forward your proposed questions so there are no surprises to either party.

Decide on a mutually convenient time.

I highly recommend using Skype video for your interviews it's free for both parties and in order to record the interview all you need is a simple app that integrates directly into Skype. These apps are very easy to use and easy to find. For PC there is VodBurner and for MAC there is eCamm.

Finally you will need a simple web cam but most laptops these days have an inbuilt camera that will do the job.

Once the interview is done prepare a full transcript for those people who prefer to learn by reading rather than watching a video.

Prepare a package of 4 or 5 interviews in both video and .pdf format (transcript of the video interview).

You now have your very own product to sell.

Create a squeeze page offering one of your video interviews as your free offer in return for emails addresses.

On the download page presell your complete interview package.

Create your sales page.

Next get the link to your squeeze page out there.

Use forum signatures, Facebook, Twitter, ask your friends to send the link to their Facebook page etc.

If you have a little money to invest in your business, I highly recommend that you invest in a couple of solo ads or ezine adverts.

Only choose ones that exactly match your product content. It's no good advertising in a writer's ezine if your interviews are about making money on Facebook.

Once you begin to get subscribers to your list, you can sell your complete product after a few informative emails to your subscribers.

5 Simple OFFLINE Money Machines that Pay You Month After Month

Introduction

In this section you will learn 5 Simple OFFLINE Money Making Methods that will pay you over and over **but** you will be required to do the initial work to secure the contract.

Now you are going to tell me that you:

- …don't like speaking to people on the phone – I've got you covered.

- …don't like cold calling – I've got you covered.

- …don't know anything about offline marketing – I've got you covered.

- …don't know what to offer a small business – I've got you covered too.

In this section we will be putting together a few income streams that can make you a very nice recurring income. We will be securing monthly contracts from small businesses who need your help.

Don't panic – you don't need to get suited and booted and hit the streets if you would rather not do that. I will be showing you a few ways to secure those contracts from home.

Contrary to some of the internet marketing hype that you see everywhere, there are no instant or 'push button' money makers. But the 'offline' method is responsible for lots of people making big bucks for minimum effort.

It may take a little time before the money starts coming in, but it will – if you are persistent.

Again, these methods should only take around an hour or two each day to implement once you have secured the contract, so you should still have the time to work any other jobs you may want to be involved in. but the more time you devote to 'offline' marketing, the more money you will make.

As before, these methods are scalable, which means that you can add to them and increase the frequency you do them allowing you to increase the amount of money you receive each month.

The beauty of 'offline' marketing is the opportunity to have small business owners pay you every month in return for your help in increasing their profits.

Remember, the average small business owner knows very little about online marketing so you are easily able to position yourself as the expert in your field and make yourself the 'go to' person for all their online requirements.

One important thing I need to point out is, **only promise what you can deliver.** Don't offer to increase their business by 50% (or whatever…), but offer to help them increase their business.

Offline Method 1

This method is a great, easy way to make some extra cash, even if you have never tried selling your online expertise to offline businesses.

It is a great way to begin your offline marketing career because it is usually an easy sell and you don't spend time doing anything until you have closed the sale. The potential client soon realises what good you can do for their business.

This method will give you confidence if this is your first time cold calling, when you realise how simple it is to close a sale offering this simple, one-off service.

It also gives you a foot in the door to offer more services to the client who has already seen what great things you can do for them.

You are going to be creating a simple, short video to showcase your prospects business.

Don't Panic – I'll show you how to do it; it's easy!

For this method, it works best if you have an ipad or a tablet. I would suggest a big one, around a 9 -10 inch screen.

If you only have a laptop, you could use that but it works best if you can hand the computer to your prospective client for him to hold because they tend to pay more attention if they are the one holding the equipment.

You also need to have a simple movie editing software, there is usually one already installed on your PC that will do the job (Windows Movie Maker).

If you have a good digital camera that is able to take decent quality pictures, that's ideal. But, if not, a lot of mobile phones have good, high quality cameras these days.

If you don't have this or similar equipment, borrow from someone, or use cheaper equipment and charge a little less for your service until you can afford higher-quality equipment.

There are 2 ways to make your very first sample video that you will show to future prospects.

1. Choose a restaurant local to you that you are familiar with; maybe one that you frequent yourself.

Check out their website to see if they have a video or photos of the interior of their business.

If they don't, phone or call round in person (good practise for later when you are actually selling your service...) and ask if they will let you take some photographs of their premises.

Tell them that you are going to use these photo stills to create a short video of their restaurant interior and they are welcome to use this on their website.

You could also include a photo or two of the restaurants 'signature dishes' if they would like you to.

Avoid taking your photos when the restaurant is open with customers as you may be required to get signed releases from the customers in order to use your photographs.

There will, of course, be no charge to this restaurant as long as they are happy for you to use their video as a sample to show to other business owners.

Make sure the video has a title slide to introduce the restaurant you are promoting with an additional slide at the end of the video with the address and phone number on it. If the restaurant has a logo – use that too.

You could use a shot of the outside of the restaurant with text added to the photo saying something like:

"Click to Take a Look inside XXXX Restaurant"

Clicking on the video will cause it to play.

If you are not sure how to create a video using Windows Movie Maker, do a search on YouTube for tutorials – it really is simple even for a beginner.

Send the video to the restaurant owner for his approval and tell him he is welcome to upload it to his website.

Ask for a testimonial.

However, he may want you to upload the free video to their website or to some of the video sharing sites. If so, you can charge a small fee for this service.

2. Go to Google image search, or to a photo stock website, and search for restaurants.

Download a few good pictures of restaurant interiors. Ten photos would make a video of approximately one minute duration.

Copyright is not really an issue here as you are not intending to publish them anywhere; you will simply be using them to show your prospective clients.

However, if you intend to put the resulting video on your own website to showcase your service you must get the necessary permissions to use the photos.

There are quite a few websites that allow you to use their photos for free.

5 Simple Money Machine Series ©L J Samuels

Edit the images together creating a sample video around 1 minute long, with sliding images. Don't go mad on the editing – simple is better.

Make it look professional. Add some music that you think fits the ambience of the restaurant.

Again, you can search online for free music to use.

When you're done creating the video to use as your showcase, transfer the video to your ipad/tablet.

Now it's time to sell your service.

Find some local restaurants. Make a note of likely businesses to target as you drive round your locality. Do a search on Google for 'restaurants in [your area]' Use the yellow pages online to find contact details and make a note of the ones that have websites.

Look at their websites, and see if they have any images of the inside of the restaurants. If not, these are the ones you will target.

If they don't have a website – make a separate note of these for future reference. (See Method 3)

Take your ipad/tablet and camera and visit these restaurants. A personal visit is so much more productive than a phone call because the prospect can see that you have everything ready for him to see what you are proposing, so it is more difficult for them to put you off.

Ask for the manager/owner. If he's not in, try and make an appointment or just call back later.

If you get to see the owner, tell him you found out about their restaurant from their website, and you noticed they didn't have any images showing the inside of the restaurant. Tell him that the inside of a restaurant is important to customers. They care about how it looks and feels. And if they have seen it, they are more comfortable going there.

We have all turned up at an unknown restaurant to find it is in need of redecoration, not as clean as it could be etc. I vividly remember a restaurant in Paris – but that is another story…

Tell him you have a solution. You can take some pictures of the inside of the restaurant, and create a short movie which gives their customers a feeling of how the restaurant is, and that you brought with you a sample video so they can see how the video of their restaurant could look.

Show him the sample video on your ipad/tablet; let the owner hold it whilst watching. It feels better holding it, and the video gets much more attention and makes an impression.

Try to make the owner understand how great it would be to have a video like that on their restaurant's website, so everyone who visits will be able to watch it and instantly get a good impression and feeling about their restaurant.

Remember to tell the owner that you could also include some pictures of their 'signature dishes' so prospective customers can also see the great food they offer.

If your sample video is for an actual restaurant, tell them that this video is from the interior of xxxxx restaurant and is already on their website. Show him your testimonial if you managed to get a good one. No-one wants to think they are trailing behind the competition.

Then you can discuss the price.

The first time you can start low, offering to do this for $50 to $100. Tell your prospect that you will do it for them for this low introductory price in return for a testimonial.

You could also have a scale of fees depending on the length of video the client requires. The price you can charge will also depend on where you are in the world.

Collect their fee or at least a deposit before creating their video.

Go to the next restaurant on your list, and do the same thing, but you can charge more for the video as you gain confidence. You can try $200 or maybe even $500 if it's an exclusive restaurant, and you know your prospect sees the value of this service.

When you get home, you simply transfer the pictures you took of the restaurant with your camera to your computer, and edit each video like you did with the sample video.

The first time you do this, you're going to spend some time on it, making it as good as you possibly can.

You can create a template so you will have some simple effects ready to use for future videos, and have a few music tracks readily available.

You can then choose between a few different ones each time you make a video, and just add the pictures which of course, are always different.

Creating these videos can be done in no time at all once you get the hang of it. It usually takes me a maximum of 30 minutes.

Once you have created the video, send it to the restaurant owner for their approval.

You could also offer to upload it to their website, Facebook page, vimeo.com, YouTube and similar video sharing sites – for a small additional fee of course.

If you can get 5 restaurants to sign up for this service on your first day, and they pay you on average $100 each, that is $500 for only one day's work. That's not too shabby in my book!

The amount of money you can make using this method depends on how many restaurants you close, and how much you get paid.

Once you run out of restaurants in your local area, you simply move on to another area/city/state.

You could easily offer the same service to popular bars, health clubs or cafés. The only limit to your potential client base is your imagination.

A good way to get more clients in other parts of the country is to hire salespeople. You don't have to do any of the cold calling; you simply create the videos from the photos your sales people send you when they close a sale.

You could advertise on Craiglist or your local free ad paper for people to sell your service and take the photos. You would pay a commission for each sale of between 50% and 100%.

You can afford to pay 100% commission if you are confident that you can sell more of your services to the client.

This one method alone could make you a nice bit of cash – you just have to get out there and do it!

Offline Method 2

If you hate the idea of cold calling, this next method is a good place to start.

It does take a little work to set up but can prove to be very lucrative.

You will need a printer, paper, a red pen, a few cheap A4 folders with a clear front cover (you can get these from Staples or Ebay), your business card and some A4 envelopes.

The first step is to grab a few of your local newspapers and look through the classified sections.

You will see people who are already paying money to advertise their business or services.

Choose a few of these and check if they have a website and where it is in the Google search engine. (As I said in Method 1, if they don't have a website, make a note of it for future reference).

If it is a plumber, search for "plumber" + your town.

You are looking for your prospects details – ideally on page 2 or lower. If they are on page 1 with a listing in the Google Places section, move on to the next one.

Once you find a prospect that is on page 2 or lower for the keywords that someone would type into Google when looking for that type of business, cut out their advert from the newspaper.

When you have the appropriate Google page displayed on your computer, take a screen shot (simply press the button that says 'Prt Sc' on the top row of your keyboard). Go to 'Paint' which is installed on most computers, and click 'file' then 'paste'.

The Google page will show up, save this as a 'jpeg'.

Next, print out the page and put a circle round the page number and an arrow pointing to their website using your red pen. Alternatively, you can use the 'paint' tools to add your red circle and arrow as I have done in the example below.

You can see that this plumber is on page 2 of the Google search pages.

If you wanted to hammer the point home even more, you could print the first page of the search results to show how their competitors are listed in Google Places. See below:

After checking out the website I used in this example it is obvious that this one is provided by Yell Sites (yellow pages websites) so make a separate note of that, it may come in handy later on for any upsells.

Now head on over to the free Google keyword tool

www.adwords.google.com/o/**KeywordTool** and type in the search words you used before, in this case 'plumber plymouth', to show your prospect how many people are searching for his type of service or business.

Again, take a screen shot, paste into 'paint' and highlight the relevant information so it's easy to see at a glance.

See below:

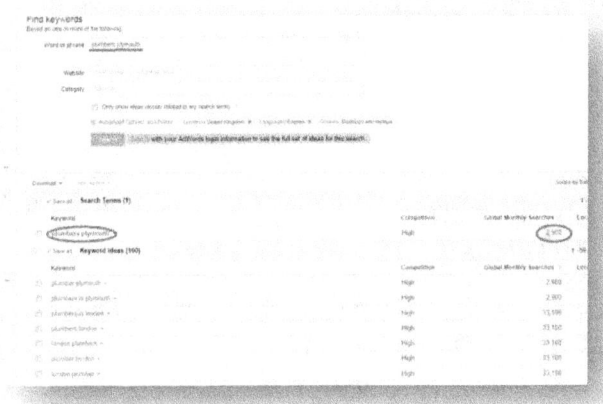

Print the page.

Right, you have all the information you need to send to the prospect except a letter explaining your proposal.

Below is a suggestion for the type of cover letter to include in your folder.

~~~~~~~~~~~~~~~~~~~~~~~~~~~~~~~~

Dear Mr Adams, [always try and find the correct name of the owner of the business]

I saw your advertisement in the [name of publication]

Are you happy with the increase in your business due to this advertisement or has the response been disappointing?

You don't need me to tell you that traditional advertising such as Yellow Pages and local newspaper adverts are not as effective as they were in the past.

Times have changed. Nowadays most people, including many of your potential clients, tend to search on the Internet for services [or businesses] such as yours.

However, when I did a simple search on Google earlier today I noticed that your website is only listed on page** [whatever page number their website is currently on**].

I have attached a print out of the Google search I used to try and find your website online using the typical search phrase that a potential customer would use when looking for your business.

The phrase I used in the Google search bar was:

- *Plumber Plymouth*

As you can see from the print out, I eventually found your website on page 2 of the Google search results.

You can try this yourself, or get somebody else to try and find your website by typing in some key phrases that your typical customer might use to search for your business.

Now, I don't know about you, but when I am looking for a local business, I rarely go beyond page 1 of the search results.

*Your competitors who currently dominate the top 3 listings in Google are ranked high because they have listed their websites in Google Places. You can see the map on the right hand side of **page 1** of the Google search results with the letters showing clients exactly where to find them.*

As you can imagine, they will be attracting the most attention from potential clients because of where they are in the search results.

*This month alone, **over (xx) people actively searched on Google for a** (their niche) **business in** (your area) **and they couldn't find your website.***

*I have enclosed a printout showing the **exact number** of **local monthly searches** for YOUR type of business.*

Although it is not too difficult to add your business to the Google Places in order to be listed along with your competitors, it is time consuming and requires some knowledge of how the search engines work in order for your website to be easily found by customers actually looking for you.

My company specialises in promoting local companies here in [the area you are covering] using the Google Places feature and lots of other methods that can greatly improve your visibility online.

If you want to know more about how I can help drive a lot more potential clients to your website every month, please don't hesitate to give me a call.

Yours sincerely,

[Your signature]

P.S If you contact me within 7 days of receiving this letter I will guarantee a 50% reduction of our rates as an introductory bonus. Act now to increase the chances that your company will be the one chosen over your competitors.

~~~~~~

Use a good quality paper with your company and contact details clearly displayed, sign the letter by hand.

Create a simple title page to include in the pack.

The Truth About

www.theirwebsite.com

Read on to see what we discovered...

Fix their advert (which you had previously cut from the newspaper) to the letter from your company with a paperclip then put everything together inside the folder.

Don't forget to add your business card.

Place into envelope and hand-write the name and address. A hand-written envelope is more likely to be opened than a printed one.

Once you have the cover letter and title page created you can save these and simply change the recipient details each time.

Aim to post 5 of these packs per day and the chances are that you will easily close a couple of sales per week.

What you can charge for this service will depend on where you are in the world. I typically charge between $397 & $767 for this service.

Once you have closed a deal, you must be prepared to do a fantastic job with this service so you can easily upsell them for more of your offerings.

Offline Method 3

This method requires that you offer prospects a free 3 page website.

Yes, you read that right – a **FREE 3 PAGE WEBSITE!**

I'm not suggesting that you work for free but you will be using this strategy to get your 'foot in the door'.

Let me ask you this:

Q. If you want a website to showcase your business or service, what do you need to make it show up online?

A. **Hosting!**

Now do you see where I'm going with this?

You will build a simple 3 page website for the client similar to the Wordpress site that I created a few years ago for a client of mine:

(it looks much better in color…)

The client continues to pay me a monthly fee for his hosting plus I was able to charge an extra flat fee for adding a 'gallery' and a 'reviews' page.

I was also paid to add his business to Google Places.

So I'm sure that, by now, you can see the benefits of offering a free website in order to secure the business.

Once I get an enquiry for the free 3 page website, I make sure that the prospect is fully aware of the fact that, for a credible online presence, they need to

100

purchase their own domain name (a one-off cost) and they will need to have hosting (recurring cost).

Most of the people that contact you will not have any idea how to organise this so this is where you will make your money.

However, if they want you to build a website then take control by hosting it themselves, move on to the next prospect – we are not interested in working for those people. We need to make a living!

Once you have a client wanting to go ahead, the first step is to buy the domain name, I use GoDaddy but you may have another preference. I buy the domain through my own account so I have full control of it until the client has paid me.

If you use GoDaddy, don't forget to look on Google for current promo codes to reduce the cost.

A good idea is to try and buy a generic local domain, for example: 'plymouthplumber.co.uk' or .com or 'plumberinplymouth.co.uk etc.

This means you will be minimising the risk of being left with a useless domain name if the prospect doesn't pay the bill. You will be able to sell it to another 'plumber in plymouth', and usually for a nice profit.

It is also easier to rank a domain like that because people would usually search for 'plumber in plymouth' than 'Jones plumbers, plymouth'.

Once the domain is purchased you need to redirect it to the hosting company you are intending to use. I use Hostgator for my hosting but you use whichever hosting company you are happy with. With Hostgator you can host unlimited websites for a flat fee of around $14.

Next you need a custom header for your site. If you can make a professional one yourself, that's great. But I usually go to fiverr.com and get one made for – yep, you guessed it - $5. The one in the example above was made by a guy on fiverr.

These small setup costs will be recouped in the first month or two when they pay you the monthly hosting fee. I usually charge around $9.47 per month for hosting to be paid monthly in advance. I offer a discount for paying 3, 6 or 12 months in advance. After you have signed up the first client any subsequent clients are pure profit for you.

You will also need some copy for the home page and also for the 'about' page. Ask your client to write a few paragraphs about his business and provide you with a photograph or two of their work.

If they would rather you did it for them, charge a small fee for a short article ($5-$10) and find some free generic photos online to use.

You now have everything ready to put together a simple site. I use Wordpress.org because you can easily give your client the login details to their website to make changes or to add information if they want.

But most will want you to do everything for them, including adding posts and more pages etc. This is an extra service that you can charge a fee for.

When building the free site, use the default Wordpress theme so it is simple to add your custom header and edit the colors. Create two extra pages 'about' and 'contact'. For the 'contact' page use the 'contact7' plugin.

Make sure you set the 'home' page as the static front page within the 'settings' tab of the Wordpress dashboard.

Once you have done a couple of these simple sites, it should take no more than 30 minutes to set up once you have all the material collected.

To get clients you could advertise in your local free press, the local newspaper, Craigslist, Gumtree etc.

You should get quite a few enquiries – everyone loves the idea of getting something for nothing.

But do make sure that your prospects are absolutely clear of the small on-going costs (hosting) and the small set-up costs (domain purchase, content creation etc.) before you begin any work. You don't want them to be under the impression that it doesn't cost anything at all to have an online presence.

This is a service that you can offer to clients who live anywhere in the world – there is no limit!

Offline Method 4

This method requires a bit more work on your part before you begin to see a profit.

You are going to buy a good local domain name. For example, one that is available as I write this is

plumberinpittsburgh.com

Once you have bought your domain you need to build a simple website. Three pages should be enough.

You need to write (or have someone write for you) a 500 – 800 word article using your keywords as the title of your article. The keywords should also appear in the first line of the article.

For Example: **"Plumber in Pittsburgh – What to Look For.**

When looking for a Plumber in Pittsburgh, these are a few things you need to consider…blah, blah…"

Make sure your keyword phrase appears a few more times throughout the article without it sounding too contrived.

Add some photos using your keyword phrase as the "alt" tag.

Next you need to rank the website on the first page of Google search results. This is usually quite easy using a local domain name and local keywords.

Add your website to Google Places and get lots of one way backlinks.

For the one way backlinks you need to spend time adding your website to lots of business directories and maybe building a few free websites containing a link to your website. You can use Squidoo, Wordpress.com, Blogger, Tumblr etc. for this.

Once your site is indexed, you can also add your article to some of the more popular article directories.

It may take a few weeks to get the website in the top few on Google search, but once you have done that, you are now the proud owner of some valuable real estate.

Now it's time to contact some prospects in order to sell them advertising on your site.

Check out your local newspaper and Yellow Pages to find, in this case, Plumber in Pittsburgh. The reason we use these methods to find prospects is that they are already paying for advertising.

We would then send them a simple email as follows:

~~~~~~~~~~~~~~~

Hello,

My company has a #2 ranked website, http://yourwebsite.com

It is highly optimized and currently holds a great position above Google Places on the search pages for the keyword:

"Plumber in Pittsburgh".

This is the phrase that someone who is looking for your service would type into the search engine and our website is right there for them to see.

At the moment our website is getting XXX visitors per week, all looking for your service.

We rent ad space on this website and currently have a premium position available. Each day this site is found by users in Pittsburgh who are looking for a plumber.

We build and optimize websites for professionals to attract highly targeted potential customers and offer competitive rates for monthly advertising.

To discuss rates, find out about our 'two for one' offer or reserve your space today, please reply to this email or call me directly at, [your phone number]

Regards,

[your name]

~~~~~~~~~~~~~~~~~~~~

I would usually only allow one or at the most, two Plumbers [or Mortgage Brokers etc.] to advertise on my website and collect a nice monthly payment from them.

Obviously for any business that wants to advertise on your site exclusively the monthly rate would be higher.

When selling the advertising space, focus on the number of visits your site gets – you can supply proof by sending screenshot of your website stats to anyone who shows an interest.

Your prospects couldn't really care less where your site is positioned on Google if you don't get any visitors – so hammer that point home.

To sweeten the deal I usually offer the first two months advertising for the price of one month.

Once you have agreed terms, you would ask them for a banner for your site to advertise their services. If they don't have one available, you can offer that service as well. Get a banner made on Fiverr and charge your client around $20 - $40 for this service. Or, if you are good at graphic design, you can make one yourself.

If an advertiser fails to pay for their advertising space, send them one reminder then, if they don't pay up, simply remove their banner and move on to the next prospect.

Once you have one high ranking website with lots of visitors, buy your next domain name and 'rinse and repeat'.

Simple!

Offline Method 5

For this method we are going to show clients how to get customers through the door by offering discounts and doing regular, simple promotions.

Almost everyone these days has a smart phone and we are going to use this and the QR code app to collect customer's information.

The general idea of this method is to collect the customers email address. Once we have this information, it is easy to send details of imminent promotions to entice customers to the premises on slow days.

First you need to create a sample campaign to show to prospects.

So, on a 'throw away' domain or a sub-domain set up a simple squeeze page asking people to enter their email address.

You don't need their name, just keep it simple.

The squeeze page would contain copy something like this:

We at XXXX regularly have very special discount offers for our VIP customers.

To join XXXX Discount Club and make sure you get the special codes to claim your EXCLUSIVE DISCOUNTS, fill in your email address below.

Email: _____

Enter your email address today and you will receive a special discount code for $2 [or whatever] **off your next order at XXXXX**

Obviously you will need an autoresponder service to collect the email addresses.

Next create a QR code using the URL of your squeeze page as the destination.

You can create a simple one for free. Below is just one of the sites that offer a free QR code creator.

www.unitaglive.com/qrcode

This is a QR code I created for my own squeeze page which offers a free report.

(this is a bright red color)

Test it out so you know how a QR code works.

If you haven't already got it, you will have to download the QR reader app to your phone. Then simply point and click (a bit like taking a photo) to be taken straight to my squeeze page.

You are welcome to fill in your email address to claim the free report that is offered on the page. ☺

Next, set up your autoresponder with a follow-up email to be sent immediately (day 0). The email should contain a code for the customer to redeem whatever was promised in the opt-in form.

So the email could read something like:

~~~~~~~~~~~~~~~

Welcome to XXXXXX Discount Club.

We are excited that you have decided to join our VIP customers.

Whenever we have a special offer running we will make sure that you will be one of the first to know so you don't miss out.

Check your email regularly to see our latest offers and promotions.

As promised, in return for you entering your email address today we are offering you the opportunity to get your 20% discount on any order over $10 [or $2 off, free dessert, free bottle of house wine etc.] on your next visit to the restaurant.

Simply quote the reference '20EMAIL' when you call to book your table [pay for your...].

If you don't quote the reference number when booking [at the checkout] you will not be able to claim your exclusive discount.

This offer is valid any evening [a quiet time] between 6pm and 9pm.

We look forward to seeing you.

Best regards

XXXXXXX

~~~~~~~~~~~~~~~~~~

You are now ready to search for potential clients to offer this service to.

Print out your QR code.

You could begin with restaurants and takeaway businesses local to you.

Choose a time when you know the business will be quiet and call in. Ask to see the proprietor.

If he can't see you, make an appointment.

If you do get to see him, tell him how you can show him a simple way to get more customers through the door on his quiet days.

You are going to show him your sample squeeze page. Get him to scan the code and sign up so he can see the follow-up email.

Explain that you will do all the work for him, he will simply email you the offer and code that he wants you to use 48 hours before he wants to begin his offer.

It really won't take much to close the sale because most business owners will be able to see the advantages of being able to contact people who have expressed an interest in receiving his offers.

You will set up his squeeze page, set up a dedicated list within your own autoresponder and set up the follow-up email as above.

Tell him that there is a one-off fee for the set-up of this service. Or you could set it up for free if you think that will seal the deal. You will make money once the service is up and running.

You could either charge a monthly fee to administer the discount club or charge per offer sent.

Your client needs to inform his staff about the new Discount Club and how it will work so the customers will get the promised discount when they give the code for the offer.

Now you need to show him how he will get people to sign up for the Discount Club.

Once you have created his squeeze page, create a QR code for him to display in his premises. He can offer customers a free glass of wine or free salad in exchange for them signing up – whatever it takes.

Place an advert in the local free newspaper with the QR code attached as well as the raw URL, an advert on the local Craigslist pages, a poster in the window of the premises, flyers on tables, for a takeaway put up posters in the local college etc.

Remember to tell people how to get the QR code app on the posters, flyers etc. so they can scan the code. But do include the full URL for anyone who would rather just type in the address.

Use your imagination to think of ways to get people to scan the QR code.

You can offer to do all this for a one-off fee.

Each time the business has a discount to offer, he would email you with the details and you would simply send the email to the list. If he is paying you per email, make sure he sends payment before you send the email. If he is paying a monthly fee, collect the payment monthly 'in advance'.

The beauty of this is, if the client bales on you, you still have a list of potential clients for restaurants or takeaway establishments that could be used for marketing other similar businesses.

So, for you, it's a win – win situation if you keep control of the list.

Once you get a couple of these 'offline' systems up and running you can use outsourcers to do the work for you if you like.

Things like building backlinks, writing articles, SEO etc. can all be successfully outsourced freeing up your time to sell more of your services.

Offline marketing can be very lucrative and hundreds of marketers enjoy a very good lifestyle once they have built a client base who will automatically pay monthly fees for your service.

You could be one of these people…

Please don't just think about it - do it!

I hope this book has provided you with some useful ideas to make money from home.

As I have said previously, absolutely nothing will happen if you don't DO something.

Most of the methods in this book are easily achievable by anyone – I recently had a 17 year old email me to say he had made his first $125 implementing just one of the methods.

I wish you every success in your career and remember, you are the only one who has any control over your success or lack of it.

It's time to go and create your own Pot of Gold.

"The difference between a successful person and others is not a lack of strength, not a lack of knowledge, but rather a lack in will."

~ Vince Lombardi

"So the only way on earth to influence other people is to talk about what they want and show them how to get it."

~ Dale Carnegie